DREAM SPELLS

DREAM S PELLS

Understanding Your Dreams

C L A I R E   N A H M A D

Illustrations by Juliette Pearce

PARKGATE
BOOKS

DEDICATION

To the memory of Nathan Chapman and his baby sister, Paige
"Our greater reality lies beyond our brief dreamlike spell on
this earth." (Sarah Greaves)

First published by Pavilion Books Limited, 1994
This edition published in 1998 by

Parkgate Books Ltd
Kiln House
210 New Kings Road
London SW6 4NZ
Great Britain

1 3 5 7 9 8 6 4 2

Copyright © Pavilion Books Limited, 1994
Illustrations copyright © Juliette Pearce, 1994
Text copyright © Claire Nahmad, 1994

British Library Cataloguing in Publication Data:
A catalogue record for this book is available from the British Library.

ISBN 1 85585 538 0

Designed by Nigel Partridge

Printed and bound in China
by Sun Fung Offset Binding Company Limited.
Produced in association with the Hanway Press, London.

CONTENTS

INTRODUCTION

ℋARP OF ℧ILD AND DREAMLIKE STRAIN'

*𝒯*he title of Emily Brontë's evocative poem could almost be a hymn to the Moon, for it asks the question

. . . When I touch thy strings,
Why dost thou repeat again
Long-forgotten things?

The Celtic lunar goddess Ahrianrad might be able to reply, for it is she who holds in her hands the silken threads of humanity's inner soul-life, upon which she plays to weave the subtle web of destiny, dreams and visions which comprise her domain. She is the Moon, the Lunar Woman, and the wisdom of the ancients tells us that the tides of light and shadow of which human beings are made flow through us ceaselessly, and that whilst the conscious, rational, everyday self is ruled by the Sun, our converse, deeper aspect comes under the sovereignty of Selene or Luna, the Moon goddess. She rules the soul and the memory and their emotional waters which are both refined and turbulent, high and low in scale. That deep surging ocean is the sea of Life itself, from which all creation eventually emerges into the sunlight. It is into the hushed echoing deeps of those fathomless waters that we return each night, to experience 'the little death'. Later, when the time is ripe, we withdraw entirely into the sanctuary of the inner worlds to seek the adventure of fresh challenge and self-realization, a fate which humanity calls 'death'.

○   ○   ○

As mistress of Vision and goddess of Dreams, we could learn much from the Moon goddess of our own inner nature

and soul-forces by deciding to respond creatively and
consciously to our dreams. Generally, we tend to keep
Luna's precious secrets locked away from ourselves, and
take no heed of the nightly voyages we make into her
strange worlds, which are filled with wisdom and beauty,
qualities we can well perceive by learning such simple
techniques as dream-continuation, recall and re-entry which
are described in these pages. The 'fruits and flowers' of
dreams which are the measure of enlightenment and renewal
which can come to our outer daily lives when we begin to
converse and commune with the Moon goddess of sleep
cannot be thought of merely as enhancement. Our dreams
contain the essence of that which is profoundly vital in the
establishment and maintenance of beautiful and harmonious
living, so that we may be at peace with the outer
community because we are at peace with ourselves. If there
is, as some say, a 'Dreamer dreaming us', then it would
seem consistent to believe that the mysterious process we
call dreaming, both asleep and awake, contains the veritable
secret of Creation itself.

○   ○   ○

If the Moon is indeed Mistress of Dreams, and wields the
Wand of Vision, we may learn much from contemplating
the wonderful story of Endymion and the Moon from
ancient legend. The mythic sequence is that Luna the Moon
woman, ascending her astral stairway like a dove, came one
night upon Endymion, the Shepherd of Nature (a symbol for
humankind, in its role as steward of the planet) as he lay
sleeping. She fell in love with him, but found that she could
possess him only when he slept; therefore, she set out to
enchant him so that she could reach his soul during the day
as well as at night, her own domain. This old tale seems to
corroborate in mystical terms the archetypical idea that the
Dreams of Endymion are valuable assets to our waking
hours as well as to those spent asleep. We must learn to
'wake within sleep' and, like Endymion, 'watch the bright
rivers of our dreams' even as we voyage out upon them. In
the Moon woman's world, everything is possible, especially

to be an observer and a participant simultaneously. Sleep is a source of refreshment and revitalization not only for our physical bodies, but also for those much finer, more subtle bodies of mind, emotion and spirit.

○ ○ ○

Many figures in mythology play upon magical harps whose lovely strains send their listeners deep into the underworld of sleep, there to follow a magical pathway of dreams whose messages are treasured as wise teachings. The Moon is said to be a great gateway 'of pearls and crystal, ivory and horn' through which we wend our way each night to the shining lands of the soul; to her belongs the past and all secrets and mysteries. Perhaps this vision of her would frame the best answer to Emily's haunting lines 'Why dost thou repeat again/Long forgotten things?'

THE DREAM VOYAGER

And it shall come to pass in the last days, sayeth God, I will pour out my spirit upon all flesh; and your sons and your daughters shall see visions, and your old men shall dream dreams.

ACTS ii, 17

*T*he ancient alchemists, who through the ages sought the living gold secreted in the heart of dull matter, proclaimed that when the body slept, the soul awakened. Carl Jung, the famous psychologist, described the dream as a miraculous little door, hidden deep in the secret chamber of our innermost selves, which opened on to the fathomless night of humanity's larger being. This strange night was illuminated by the beautiful and ineffable light of the moon, the stars and radiant nebulae, as is the night which falls upon our physical world, for the outer world perceived through the five senses is but an echo in matter of our inner reality.

o   o   o

We might think of our everyday self as being our 'Sun self', positive, rational and conscious to deal with the practical aspects of physical life. Our dreaming self is our 'Moon' or 'lunar self', receptive, reflective and active in the hours of darkness when we, and nature, sleep. The soul, symbolized by the Moon, is mistress of this inner world which is the dwelling-place in our being of memory, emotion, feeling and sensation, habits and attitudes of mind, of the sensibility which receives and responds to the constant stream of impressions that is the harvest of our everyday experience.

So that a proper balance may be maintained between these solar and lunar lifestreams which comprise our being, it is important to regard the inner worlds as an objective reality in which our subjectivity, or individuality, is rooted and nourished. Yet it is also true that we are creators of ourselves, that our life is our child, malleable, impressionable and alive to the guidance and influence of wise parenting. How therefore, can we best learn to shape our deeper selves so that we may gain ascendancy over our lives and steer our own destiny?

The answer might well lie in accepting the idea that the soul-wisdom and visions which arise from our lunar selves can revitalize our often parched and arid outer selves. Without the Moon and the mercy of the swelling waters she commands, the Sun can cause drought and suffering. To listen to our dreams is to give ear to the life of the soul, so that its inspiration might be brought through into our everyday lives and given full expression therein. When our conscious self penetrates our dreams, and our dreaming self is allowed to participate actively in our waking lives, we strike a balance between Sun and Moon, and heal the division in ourselves which so often causes life to seem drab and meaningless. So we steer a course that lies 'east of the Sun, west of the Moon', that magical way which, according to the old tales and myths of folklore, will lead us to the Grail Castle.

DREAM TYPES

It is said that there are five types of dreams: the physical dream, the confused dream, the subjective dream, the prophetic dream and the spiritual dream. The quintessence of dreams is always fluid in nature, so even the different dream types flow in and out of one another. However, one of the above categories will characterize most dreams that occur.

○　　○　　○

The physical dream is the type favoured by the theories of the British specialist, Dr Christopher Evans. His philosophy is that dreams are a result of the biological computer which is the brain, revising and reorganizing its programmes so that they are kept synchronized and relevant for our day-to-day living. The physical dream is defined by its muddled meaninglessness and its random and mundane imagery. Physical dreams will often be provoked by illness or indisposition. The confused dream is the type which discharges a host of rapidly changing images as if the recipient were looking out of a window on a fast train journey. These images are often worth recording and studying. The subjective dream is that which derives its imagery from those scenes and persons familiar to the waking life of the dreamer. The prophetic dream gives prescience of dramatic events in the near or distant future, and delivers its message either through literal imagery or by means of symbols. The spiritual dream is a direct experience of inner subjective reality, and deep lessons of wisdom and enlightenment may be drawn from it. The prophetic dream and the spiritual dream are those most likely to speak to the dreamer through the exquisite spiritual language of symbols or Jung's archetypes. They contain dream-pictures so vivid and mythical that their meaning is instantly recognizable (such as the Madonna, the Sorcerer, the Demon, the Angel, the Hero and so on). The last three types of dream are the most valuable, especially the spiritual dream, which comprises a beautiful and precious gift to the dreamer.

The BENEFITS *of Keeping a* DREAM JOURNAL

This is best done in two stages: keep a notebook and pen by your bed and, immediately on waking, write down in sequence, everything you can remember of your dream. Try particularly to capture the emotional atmosphere emanating from dream landscapes and dream figures in your description, as well as the general feeling or tone of the dream as a whole. Was it threatening, frustrating, magical, poetic or urgent? Did it impart a sense of discovery, wonder, anger, comedy or emotional discomfort? If sexual, was it lewd or inspiring, comforting or disturbing? In the evening, enter your dream in your journal, which should be big enough to provide plenty of space for creativity. If you care to be elaborate, the following esoteric directives from the past might help you.

Queen of Sheba and King Solomon Dream Spell

When you dream with your spirit, the Sun and the Moon
are holding court within you, and it is right that you should
pay heed. Record your dreams in a journal, for when you
tell them over to yourself, you are holding communion with
your own soul. It is as if King Solomon as your waking self,
and the Queen of Sheba as your dreaming soul, held counsel
together; and indeed, the mystery of their wisdom-sharing
was this, that they were signatures for the daylight self and
the eternal soul, which should always be in deep and tender
communication, ever creating one another anew. The spirits
of King Solomon and the Queen of Sheba should therefore
preside over your journal as its guiding daemons, and the
tome itself should be dedicated to the Angel Iachadiel, who
will speak to you in your sleep.

Bind your book by hand in cloth which is of a design that
your soul delights in, and also the colours thereof. Scent its
pages by anointing their borders with rosemary oil, and
enclose lavender between some of its leaves so that it may
be crushed; for lavender and rosemary speak of invocation
and remembrance, so that what is secreted in your heart of
hearts may be summoned into the waking present, such is
the bittersweet magic of these fragrant herbs. Press a clover
leaf and one of vervain, and secure the first inside the front
cover and the last inside the back cover likewise, for then
your book will be sealed and protected by herbs holy and
sacred. Burn a white candle whilst you write your dreams
within its pages, and let it be a treasure store for all their
fruits and flowers, whether these be pictures, poesy, or
song. So will magic herbs enchant your journal with their
fragrance, and angels and ancient spirits illuminate your task
with their blessings.

Call this volume the *Book of the Firmament Within*, for such is
the realm of the dream.

○   ○   ○

Record the date and the time of your dream (as far as you
can tell upon waking) in the notebook kept by your bed,
and it is a good idea also to number it, as dream sequences
often appear in what seem at first to be random patterns.
These sometimes occur over a number of days or weeks,
depending upon the revelation the dream is attempting to
impart. Note the colours in your dream, its characters and
scenery, its imagery and symbols. Write in full any words
spoken, songs, poems or riddles. These usually occur in the
form of an absurd question which often proves to be a
mirror-image of wisdom in that the answer prompted by it
may be applied with profit to outer waking circumstances.
Be alert to the dreaming mind's love of puns, literal images
relating to figurative speech ('he talks his head off', for
instance) and its tendency to convey its truths through
jokes. For example, a man dreamed of an apple pie filled
with sour, unripe apples. His pet-name for his wife was
'sweetie-pie' and the dream pointed to her frustration at his
complacency with their superficial relationship!

Dreams seem to set a puzzle for the dreamer, and it is in
the act of analysis that many messages and revelations are
made clear. To interpret such revelations requires a
meditative and receptive level of thinking which modern-day
living tempts us to neglect. When the dreams of each night
are finally entered into the dream journal, progressive study
will prove to be exciting, edifying and revelatory. Do not
hesitate to interpret your dreams in the light of recent and
future problems and situations and the inner queries they
prompt, such as 'how can I manage to cope with this?'
Esoteric lore assures us that spirit-guides, benevolent angels,

our loved ones who have 'died', as well as the wisdom of our own soul and the symbolic archetypes it can embody and express through the medium of visions, speak to us in and through our dreams.

Always write down your dreams immediately upon waking, because they fade with such great celerity. If you perform some other task first, they will be lost to you.

How to ASK for a DREAM to be GIVEN as a GIFT

This has been practised since the beginning of time, and was anciently called 'dream incubation'. A religious shrine or some other mystical place was sought, where the dreamer would prepare him or herself for sleep as a holy ritual. The dream and its message would be imparted by either a god, a mythological beast, an angel or a spirit, depending upon the dedication of the shrine. An old dreaming spell offers a simpler ritual. Before trying the spell it is important to relax by gently focusing on the incoming and outgoing breath. Soothe away tension in the body by tightening each set of muscles in procession from the feet upwards, holding the tension for a few seconds, and then letting go. Relax the mind by slowly counting backwards from twenty. When you reach seventeen or sixteen, just cease all mental effort and let the numbers and the task simply drop away from the mind. Relax them out of consciousness, so that they are no longer important. Being now in the requisite receptive, reflective mood of mind which is the lunar spirit, you are ready to work dream magic!

Dreaming Spell

At Gabriel's third hour, which is eight o'clock in the evening, retire alone to your chamber and light a white or a silver candle. Burn some sweet herbs in a crystal incense dish and watch the Moon as she rises, if the season be right; if it is summer, contemplate the drifting clouds in their peaceful majesty. The world of legend, myth, dream and fairy-tale can be seen in the clouds.
Intone these ritual words to the Moon:

Mother Moon, Sovereign of Sleep
True and pure my visions keep.

And then to the great Angel Iachadiel:

Angel Iachadiel,
Bless this ancient dreaming spell.

And to Brigit, Dream Goddess of the Celts:

Brigit bright, give me this night
A dream to meet my soul's deep plight;
Unveil my mystic inner sight
Dispense your visions abrim with light.

Bow three times to the Moon, and then to east, west, north and south. Contemplate the candleflame glowing in the magical silence of your chamber, and let your final invocation be to the Egyptian goddess Sekhmet, The Lady of Flame and the great Seer by night:

Sekhmet, Lady of Flame,
This spell I work in your sacred name
Usher my dreams to my waking mind
So by day my soul I may find.

Snuff out the flame as your lips utter the last word of the spell, and go at once to bed, being sure to place a white rose on the left-hand corner of your pillow.
Finally, recite the rune:

May this place Shrine of Ceridwen be
And all her shining Company.

Thus you are assured that you will sail out upon the waters of your soul as a mariner of dreams, and return from your voyage with precious cargo which may be unloaded in the harbour of your waking self.

○   ○   ○

If you find the entire ritual of this Victorian dreaming spell somewhat daunting, do at least try saying the runes over to yourself before sleeping. Rhyming and magic are closely associated, and invocations in the form of a verse, however they may partake of the essence of 'cutler's poetry', are usually more effective than a request to the dreaming mind framed in plain prose. Choose any method which suits you, however, and don't be discouraged if you fail in capturing your dreams on the first night of asking. Just ask again the following night – your dreams *will* respond to your request to salvage them, even if you have never previously been able to remember them.

How to USE the DREAMING PROCESS as THERAPY

(The Prince of Enchanters Dream Spell)

Light a blue candle at Raphael's hour, which is the hour before midnight, and say this prayer:
'Merlin, Prince of Enchanters, send one of your willing servants to visit me in this night's dream. May I be healed, made whole and pure. Send sons of the flame to cleanse me by night, and daughters of wisdom to bring me knowledge of a cure I may take in my waking hours.'

Angel Raphael, heed my prayer
Heal me with thy Staff of Air.

Go at once to bed, and there you shall fall into a healing sleep, as if angel voices sang a lullaby. Note your dreams well, for in them a message will be imparted to you; and if you pay heed, your health and happiness shall be miraculously restored.

o   o   o

There are many reported instances of healing through the agency of dreams; sometimes famous figures from the past such as Paracelsus or Hippocrates converse with the sufferers in their dreams, enlightening them as to an actual cure; or they will dispense healing forces into the aura of patients as they sleep. One woman, who suffered from exhaustion and poor immunity, thought she had read in some ancient scripts concerning the history of Pharoah Amenhotep IV that she was studying, that an efficacious method for restoring depleted strength was to bathe in the sea each morning. The woman did so, and in a short time regained perfect health. On trying to find the directives in the scripts and being entirely unable to do so, it came to her in a flash that she had actually dreamed of the advice! The Egyptian Sun god Ra had appeared to her and supplied her with the necessary instructions to effect her recovery.

o   o   o

The ancient British mage Agrippa, who worked with angels and spirits, and who created a sacred seal of healing, also frequently appears to physically distressed people in their nightly dreams.

An EXAMPLE of DREAM INTERPRETATION

If a problem is psychological, it is worth dwelling at some
length on the signs and symbols which appear in the dreams
you request for healing. For instance, you might see a
tethered horse. The horse is a sign for energy, but as a
symbol its meaning penetrates many levels. It is a good idea
to enquire into myth and legend, for these stories are
valuable repositories of the universal secrets which stir
among the hidden depths of life, through which we can
discover objective truths, subjectively realized.

Here is how such a hypothetical dream might speak to you through its symbols: Abraxus is one of the mythical horses which draw the Dawn Chariot, and in his own right he is the spirit of each passing year. On reflection, you might decide that your problem of depression or mental exhaustion stems from the subliminal conviction that the years are not rewarding you with true progress. This could be because you are allowing some internal or external factor to stifle you and block your way, thereby 'tethering' not only your energy (the horse) but also your direction in life (Abraxus, the spirit of each passing year), and so preventing any sense of new beginnings. Once the impediment is overcome, Abraxus can once again be the dawn horse drawing the Dawn Chariot which is the vehicle of renewal and rebirth. When Abraxus is true to his own spirit, which is characterized by unfettered energy, freedom of direction, spontaneous entry into new situations and fresh challenges, your health problem will be resolved.

When examining the mythology of a symbol, always take note of those stories, legends or magical definitions which please you most and appeal to your sense of beauty and imagination. These feelings are pointers to guide you. In the supposed dream of Abraxus, for instance, there is presented to the dreamer the nature of the health problem, the deep underlying cause, and the solution to the distress, each message interwoven through this triform symbol.

Asking QUESTIONS of a DREAM

If you have a particular question, you can petition your
dreams to give you an answer. First frame your question
very clearly in your mind until it is quite definite and lucid.
Next put it to each of the deities mentioned in the *Dreaming
Spell*, so that you speak it aloud three times – if it concerns
health or healing, include Merlin or the Angel Raphael in
your invocation. An answer should come within three
nights, but again, watch out for the joking subtleties of the
dream. Bear in mind that the messenger of the Gods is the
mischievous, laughing Mercury, whose boy-spirit revels in
pranks. One woman, uncertain as to whether or not she
should quit her job for another, heard the song 'Bye Bye
Blackbird' sung to her by a dream character. The name of
her present boss was Ravenscroft – she had her answer!

Visiting OTHER WORLDS

There is an old spell for visiting other worlds in dreams.
First, however, you must decide where you want to go!
Ancient lore suggests that different worlds exist deep within
the Earth, the Moon, upon the Sun and, indeed, upon every
star and planet. Worlds existing within our own greater
consciousness occupy objective spiritual dimensions. The
world immediately surrounding the Earth-plane is the realm
of the astral, more vivid and beautiful than Earth. One can
also visit other lands on Earth in dreams. This is a form of
astral travel, but in order to be able to achieve it, the
powers of the dreaming mind, the lunar spirit, must be
invoked in the same way. As yet, of course, there can be no
objective proof that we have managed to visit other worlds.
However, it is worth noting that space photographs taken by
means of satellite stations orbiting the Earth bear an
uncanny resemblance to drawings and diagrams made by
scholars and magi of long-dead cultures, some of which
were societies so 'primitive' that they possessed no
technological knowledge.

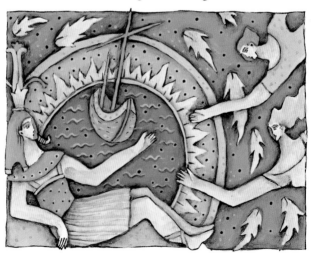

As with all spells, it is the quality of *feeling* with which we invest them that yields results. In order to ask for angelic help and guidance, it is necessary to be very still within; but at the same time, our meditations before consciously entering into the quietude of the stilled soul should be eager and enthusiastic, fostering a sense of wonder and limitless magical possibility.

The Solar Boat of Ra Dream Spell

First, you must perform the ritual dreaming spell and call upon the three deities. Afterwards, do not put out your candle, but secure it against fire and place it in the centre of your room. Walk, walk, walk around it, as the Eastern holy men do, and let it become the heart of stillness, the centre of peace. Quieten your own soul, and let the eyes of your spirit behold your wondrous destination. Now you must magically become Ra the Sun god, sailing in the heavens within his mystic solar boat. Feel this Sun boat set out upon the waters of the Soul of All Things, borne on angelic wings of shining light, and speeding to that place of which you

dream and for which you long. After perambulating for a while, sit down and study the candleflame, and grow still and hushed within. Thus calmed, you may speak quietly and serenely to the angels:

Shining Angel Sophiel
Guard my ranging soul right well;
Angel called Abariel
Bless this sea where all souls dwell;
As I sail upon its waters
Sons of Flame and Evening's Daughters
Speed my vessel on and on
Where worlds end and rise again
Michael altogether bright
Keep me on my course tonight!

Having thus petitioned the angels, you may be sure that you will travel to worlds both strange and beautiful, wherever it is your wish to go, should that be right; if it is not right, abide uncomplainingly by the wisdom of the angels who will block your way. Take courage; when the time is right, you will travel joyously, and doubly bright will be your vision of the vistas of those spiritual worlds which are of the realms of Paradise.

Whichever dreams it is your delight, or yet your sorrow, to receive from the arms of the angels, gods and spirits, give thanks in full, and from a true heart; or, it will certainly come to pass that a veil will be cast before your dreaming eyes, and you will go down into the Waters of Lethe, which are the waters of forgetfulness. Therefore, heed well these words.

HEALING *others*

It is possible to heal others in dreams. It is important to
remember, however, that we are only agents for the healing
forces of the universe, which flow forth from the angelic
stream of life. Before settling down to sleep, recite a simple
prayer to Raphael, the angel of healing, asking that you
might be allowed to visit the patient in your sleep and
dispense healing. Then visualize that person, and call them
by name into the heart of a perfect pink rose, as though the
golden stamen were an altar, and the rose petals the walls
of an exquisite temple. See the patient being healed by
angelic inspiration, deep in the heart of the rose. Calling
once more on Raphael, ask that this great healing angel
might convey your love to the patient (the supreme healing
force is love) and think of your heart as a radiant sun, warm
and golden with human love, in whose brilliant rays the
patient is tenderly bathed. Relax and go to sleep, and if you
have contacted Raphael (which you will certainly achieve if

your intentions are pure and the healing given freely as a gift of the spirit) you will help your friend, even though you may not bring the dream experience back into waking remembrance every time. If you say the prayer (which in this instance should always be in your own words) and perform the ritual conscientiously, but yet seem to be unable to attain results, it is worth examining your motives. The angels instructed wisewomen and occultists of old that they should never attempt to heal if they wished to glory in their own powers or imagine themselves to be living saints! Always try to heal without bragging or becoming convinced that you have special powers; then you may be certain that you are attuning yourself in the right way.

RESCUING *lost* SOULS

There is a place which seers call the 'Shadowland', a dark and silent astral plane which might be considered as the objectified thought-consequence of materialism. As sleep is called the 'little death', and is presided over by the Moon, so it is said that the souls of the 'dead' must pass onwards into the light through the gates of the Moon. The Shadowland is believed by some to relate to the soul-sphere directly before these gates. Souls become trapped in the Shadowland when they cannot believe in the continuum of life after death. Finding themselves still conscious and, indeed, still themselves, yet in a strange and unfamiliar world, they quite refuse to believe that they have 'died' and must move on, up and away from the Earth's sphere! Consequently, the gates of the Moon remain closed and obscured to them. Because of our prevailing rationalistic philosophy, the Shadowland is reported to be a crowded domain today, containing many confused souls who are unable to make progress. It is to this Shadowland that we

can journey by night in our dreams to help those who need
enlightenment. As you lie down to sleep, ask the Angel
Azrael to help you. State your purpose clearly and
succinctly as a prayer. Then visualize the Angel Azrael
placing a lantern into your hands (see page 41). The lantern
is a holy symbol; you have been entrusted with the care of
the Sacred Flame, and in sleep you will be led to those
bewildered and beleaguered souls who need the light of
your lantern to guide them through the gates of the Moon,
away from all earthly spheres and home into the light.

DIVINING *the* FUTURE

Because dream wisdom springs from the eternal 'now',
dreams constantly refer to the future. Sometimes your
dreams may be literally prophetic; on waking, a dream will
leave you with a distinct impression that its imagery
concerns future events. Take especial care to note down
such dreams, as they will probably arrive in sequence, and
the story they unfold will be of direct benefit in helping you
to deal with a prospective change or crisis, and will
illuminate opportunities and choices that you might
otherwise miss. Prophetic dreams also speak through
symbols, which need careful study and contemplation. In
your interpretations, make free use of your imagination and
intuition, and make enquiries of myth and folklore, for
these legends can serve as the 'rush tapers' which ferry light
into our shadows.

○   ○   ○

Colours are always important in dreams, and yet there is
such subtlety in their interpretation that there is a danger
the message may be overlooked. A table is provided for
easy reference. The list is not exhaustive, nor should it be
allowed to negate ideas and impressions of your own.

INTERPRETING *dream* COLOURS

GOLD
exalted spirituality, greatness, higher influences, treasure.

SILVER
cleanser, feminine power, divine priestess, white magic.

PURPLE
healing, higher psychic mind, royalty, power, idealism.

WHITE
purity, gifts of the spirit, higher attainments, perfection.

BLACK
dignity, royalty, instinctual energy, power of the unconscious.

RED
health, energy, life-force, strength, sex, danger, suffering.

PINK
love, nurturing, affection, warmth, romance, childhood.

YELLOW
intelligence, imagination, the power of thought, art.

GREEN
abundance, fecundity, good fortune, generosity, new beginnings.

BLUE
truth, nobility, inspiration, wisdom, occult power, protection.

BROWN
Mother Earth, fruitfulness, ripening, withdrawing, sadness.

ORANGE
jubilance, renewal, restoration, energy, drive, zest.

GREY
calm, stillness, nostalgia, sleep, confusion, dreariness.

The Staff, the Lantern and the Pouch of Sweet Herbs

O, the mind, the mind has mountains,
cliffs of fall,
Frightful, sheer, no man fathomed.

GERARD MANLEY HOPKINS

*W*iselore teaches that nightmares sometimes come to us because our higher spiritual mind, interpenetrating our earthly mind in dreams when our egotistical will is suspended in sleep, shows us a picture of how we are failing in our spiritual destiny. As we watch it unfold, this symbolic drama takes on the characteristics of a nightmare because our shortcomings are so horrifying! Therefore, it is well worth recording even the most disturbing nightmares as they can help us to recognize dream-illumination of certain spiritual tasks which need to be carried out in our daily lives.

o   o   o

Dreams never compartmentalize reality, and even though they may be specific, their deeper source is always holistic. Nightmares contain prophecies, warnings, suppressed anxieties, unrecognized fears and unharmonized desires, which can twist and snarl through our dreams in shifting shapes of natural and fabulous landscapes, beings and animals. The elemental force of a nightmare in itself, especially when it alerts our higher perceptions to unwise attitudes and false turnings in our outer lives, can often be a

cleansing, cathartic experience – a deluge which unblocks
stifled energy channels and washes away barriers and debris.
These are the healing nightmares, testified to by many
people. Cases of paralysis in particular yield to this type of
healing, on both a physical and a psychological level.

○   ○   ○

Occasionally, nightmares can be produced by a form of
psychic attack by discarnate entities (often elemental
creatures which issue from the negative and harmful
thoughts harboured in the collective unconscious of
humanity) or by vindictive thoughts purposely directed
against us. These cause agonizing fear rather than the deeply
unpleasant anxiety which constitutes the atmosphere of
other nightmares. There is a dream spell which can protect
against them:

The Incubus and Succubus Dream Spell

There are certain mind-demons who pray upon mortals as
they sleep. The creature which attaches itself to a man is
called a succubus, to a woman, an incubus. These demons
are always of the opposite sex to the one they torment, for
they are in truth an opposite spirit dwelling in our
shadowed side, a spectre which Hathor, Goddess of Mirrors,
raises before us so that we might see something of our
converse selves. We should look upon them as beautiful and
loving and dwell in spiritual harmony with them, so when
they come upon us by night as hideous, raging things,
causing pressure over the region of our hearts where in fact
they should reside in creative peace, we know that we must
call out to the angels to be healed. Here is the invocation,
which should be worked before preparing yourself for sleep:

○   ○   ○

'I do summon this night the mystic Angel Sophiel, who
stands before me in an arc of purest golden light, enfolding
me deep and safe in her radiant wings, which are of that
same brilliant illumination which flows as divine fire from
her heart. To the left is the kindly spirit Aub, the Great
Protector; to her right stands the good spirit Vevaphel,

stern yet gentle Repeller of Evil. These sacred Three
enclose my soul in a cone of sweet light from Paradise,
warm and golden. Dogs of Hades, Daughters of the Earth
and the Shadow, Children of Eternal Night, thou and thy
kin can come near me no more; for those who step into the
magic ring of golden light are transformed into creatures of
bliss who love the Light of the Godhead. I dwell in the
heart of the magical ring of light whilst I wake and whilst I
sleep. Amen.'

○   ○   ○

In peace and faith, calm your fears and listen to the hush of
the night, knowing that there is nothing to make you afraid;
for the great angel and her spirits will hold you fast in the
Light of God through the watches of the night. Nestle into
sleep as trustingly as a child in its mother's arms, and your
dreams will be of Paradise.

○   ○   ○

As always when working a dream spell, visualization of the
imagery concerned is all-important.

COMMUNION *with* DREAM FIGURES

One of the methods of Jung, further developed by Strephon
Williams of the Jungian-Senoi Institute in America, is to
initiate a dialogue with the figures from your dreams.
Having described your dream in your journal and made a
careful list of its signs, symbols and imagery, select what
seems to be a key figure (it could be a bird, a fire, a cloud
or a tree as well as a person). With pen and paper at hand,
relax and recreate the atmosphere and the energy of your
dream, perhaps closing your eyes to help the process. When
you have reconnected with the 'story' of your dream,
summon the figure with whom or which you wish to speak,
and put questions to it that will help to clarify the purpose
and the meaning of your dream. If it was a nightmare, you
might wish to enquire of the persecutor in your dream why
it should have threatened or distressed you. Enter into a
magical relationship with this dream figure where inhibitions
and constraints are dissolved or suspended. Write down the
response, bringing the communion to a natural end as you
feel it appropriate. If any dream figure fails to respond, ask
it why it refuses to do so! This will often lift a barrier.

Dream RE-ENTRY

Strephon Williams also developed a method of dream re-entry, in which the dreamer consciously recalls his or her dream. In this method, the eyes are closed to induce a meditative, dreamlike state, and the dreamer returns to the dream so that conflicts may be resolved, tensions eradicated, beginnings explored and opportunities realized. Once again, the dream scenario and its continuation have to be written down as experienced. It is a matter of calling your dream to you and letting it unfold. If the analytical brain demands too much control, the delicate links with the subconscious mind will break, and the dream will be lost, perhaps even destroyed. Yet simultaneously, it is important that the transformative power of the conscious mind and will is allowed to operate according to the purpose of the dreamer, or else the point of re-entry will not be fulfilled. During a nightmare, it is usual to wake up as the distress moves towards a climax. For nightmares and other worrying or unsatisfactory dreams, it is useful to create in your imagination a number of healing and protective tools or symbols which you can consciously carry back into the dream with you. In cases where the force of the dream awakens you in mid-stream, dream re-entry can be achieved simply by determining a plan of action which your dream-ego (your dreaming self, either in normal or other guise) will follow, selecting a magical tool to take into your dream for protection, transformation and healing, and allowing yourself to fall straight back to sleep.

MAGICAL TOOLS and SYMBOLS

THE ANGEL A beautiful being in robes of light, which change
in hue according to your soul need. See your protective
angel as benign, valorous and a spirit of Divine Love. Some
names for protective angels are: Samael (Archangel of
Mars), Kerun, Seraph, Ariel, Tharsis, Bartzachiah, Eschiel,
Ithuriel, Madimiel, Abariel, Aub, Vevaphel and Sophiel.
Summon an angel into your dream with a prayer from your
heart-mind rather than your head-mind.

THE STAFF (*the divine masculine principle*) As we take on the
sacred guise of the Pilgrim, the Wandering Hermit or the
Wayfarer (the holy traveller through waking and dreaming
life) we are given the Divine Staff. The Staff is also the
Wand and is associated with the Cord or the Girdle (sacred
to the Celts, Druids and Witches). The Girdle seals and the
Wand conducts, so the Girdle represents the feminine
aspect of the masculine Wand. The Staff is a gift of power,
of will, an implement of the higher mind. The wise use of
the staff can be of help upon our dream-way, lifting us
always into a higher consciousness and a deeper
understanding. It becomes the archetypal 'Dripping Sword',
conducting the precious oil of our soul-development into
the distilling Cup or Chalice, the Holy Grail of the heart.

○   ○   ○

The Staff, then, can be a wonderful tool for healing a
nightmare by transforming its aggressive and negative
energies. Wield it to rise above the conflict and fear on the
lower planes of your dream, so that you may be given a
mature and holistic understanding of what is going on, and
why. Wield it so that the unharmonized forces of the
dream, and their personifications, might be conducted back
to the integrating point of peace in consciousness. The
Angel of Dreams (Gabriel, the Moon Angel) gives the Staff
or the Wand into your hands.

THE TREE OF LIFE An important teaching about the Staff is that it is cut from the Tree of Life, an ancient archetype which is a mystic picture of the structure of inner and outer consciousness. This majestic symbol is a figure of perfect inner truth. Its roots are buried deep in the Underworld (the Realm of Dreams) and bound by the coils of the Plumed Serpent of Wisdom (the animating spirit of our dreams). Its branches form our Earth which is a centre for that point of consciousness that is Humanity, and which represents our waking mind. It is surrounded by totem animals and the mysterious beauty of all natural living and growing things, and reaches upwards into the eternal heavenly spheres which is the domain of spirit. The Tree of Life, or Ygraddisil as it was known to the people of the ancient Norse culture, is a rich meditative focus and a source of unending inspiration and learning. Use it as a healing symbol in dreams where death, degeneration, degradation and chaos hold sway, for it affirms and magically realizes growth into the Light.

○   ○   ○

THE LANTERN (*the Child of Light*) The greatest of the angelic gifts, the lantern is also the Chalice and the Holy Grail. The Chalice is our own human heart, which is a mystic organ, and is the 'lantern' or 'sun' of the body. As there is a spiritual Sun behind the physical Sun, so there is a spiritual heart which is signified by the bodily organ. The Lantern reveals to the pursuing shadows and phantoms that our heart is alive with the pure flame of Spirit, of the one God who is both Mother and Father. It is the living source of our divinity, imperishable and indestructible, which will carry us into the Greater Light when we 'die'. It is the seat of our true selves, our individuality, free from the confused murk of Earth. Just as 600 blossoms are needed to create one tiny drop of rose oil (the rose is an ancient emblem for the human heart) so countless earthly lives must be lived through in order to distil the ecstatic essence of the Spirit so that it may flare forth strong and undimmed. The Holy Grail is the 'cup that overfloweth with light' which is not only each human heart but the Heart of the Earth which corresponds to the Heart of God. It is an all-embracing affirmation, then, of a glorious brotherhood of Light which is the Earth, her humanity and the natural world, set as a jewel in the cosmos of outer worlds, and the inner spiritual worlds spiralling upwards to the heart of the conjoined God and Goddess. The gift of the Lantern is truly marvellous, because it is the essence of everlasting brotherhood (the word is used without any sexual connotation), and of everlasting life. It assures us that no matter what our darkness, pain and confusion, the light of the sacred heart may be lifted like a lantern to throw the silver and the gold effulgence of Truth upon our stony path. Michael, Angel of the Sun, gives this gift to us as we dream. Hold it aloft to cast light into the deepest recesses of darkness. It is the light of love, the ultimate healing symbol, the Child of Power and Wisdom, or the God and Goddess.

THE POUCH OF SWEET HERBS (*essence of the Goddess*) All that you need for your dream journey will be found in the Pouch of Sweet Herbs. The Pouch is a magical vessel, a body filled with the sweetness and magic of the Goddess. When you need sustenance, healing, wisdom, an answer to a question, comfort, guidance and vision, open up this Pouch and you will find your need supplied. Through the subtle perfume of the sacred herbs will be distilled the mind-essence of that which is necessary to you, embodying itself naturally according to the structures of your visualization and the Wisdom of the Goddess. The Angel of Venus (Anael) is the divine dispenser of this holy gift.

THE CADUCEUS (*healing*) The emblem of Raphael or Merlin, Angel of Healing, is a white wand entwined with the winged figures of two embracing serpents, one female, one male. It is a holistic symbol of Power (the progenitive powers of life symbolized by the male serpent), Wisdom (signified by the female serpent, who is the Plumed Serpent, keeper of divine truths) and the Flame of the Heart, or Love, symbolized by the white Wand. It is a figure of wholeness, stressing the one source of life of the three aspects of the Godhead. It is given by Raphael, Angel of Mercury. Use it to affirm goodness and wholeness in your nightmares; however much the creatures within them try to overwhelm you with a sense of disaster and horror, they will be driven back and transformed by the power of the Caduceus.

○   ○   ○

THE STAR-DRIFT ROBES (*vision*) These comprise the cloak you will need for your journey. You must summon the Star-Drift Robes to yourself by creative visualization, and a prayer that they might be given to you. They are iridescent and shimmering with myriad earthly and unearthly colours. In them are caught drifts of stars as if the hair of the Goddess streamed through them. Astral lights and the forms of fairies and angels weave a tapestry of mystic patterns through them. They are a sign and symbol that the universe is indeed your inheritance, and that it lives also deep within your very being. Take these robes and enfold yourself inside them. They pulsate with a glory of light, and seal you utterly from harm, yet not from sensitive response and experience. They are your heritage, and are given by the Earth Angel.

THE JEWEL (*spiritual enlightenment*) 'The jewel in the heart of the lotus' is the spiritual flame alive and exquisite in the cave of the heart. It is a diamond which reflects the hues of all precious stones, the sapphire, the ruby, the topaz, the emerald, the amethyst and the pearl. It can take any form and all forms. It throws a starry radiance like a magical ring about itself. Cassiel, Angel of Saturn, who rules time and all precious things which endure forever, gives this gift.

○   ○   ○

THE ROSE The rose speaks of the Simple Heart of Love. Pink as the flush of sunrise, the Rose unfolds to create a temple, a most holy sanctuary. Pure and rapturous, the lovely fragrance of the Rose ascends to heaven. When you offer the Rose in your dreams, you offer all that you are and all that you have in a supreme effort of self-giving, so that all inharmony, no matter how virulent or what form it takes, must be ushered into the heart of the sanctuary for healing. Offer it to images emanating hate and brutality in your dreams, or those which are heart-broken and sorrowful, and observe the result. Anael and the Spirits of Venus give the Rose into your keeping.

THE STARBOAT (*soul wisdom*) The Starboat is your vessel of adventure, and represents your greater self as voyager. You are Ra the Sun god in his solar boat. Without the Starboat (your soul) the precious spirit which is your centre could not be borne out upon the journey over the Waters of Life. The questing Pilgrim, the holy Wanderer, the Blessed Hermit and the Wise Wayfarer, would be paralysed, with all forward movement blocked. This is why the ancient ones sang in praise of the Starboat. Set a star at its prow and open its white sails to the spiced breezes of that World Without End which the dreamer truly discovers. Your Starboat can speed safely through danger and transform itself with the celerity of light or thought. Asariel, Angel of Neptune, brings this gift.

THE GOLDEN EGG This symbol illuminates the child ever present within your soul, and takes you into itself so that nothing can harm you. Use the Golden Egg to find and create a dynamic inner peace that is unassailable and everlasting. The Goddess gives this gift.

○   ○   ○

CAP AND BELLS This is the symbol of the Fool, the holy and profound Eternal Jester. African Bushmen (and many other cultures throughout history) worship the Fool, because he shows humanity its true reflection, and also because a man or woman must became a 'fool', according to what is outmoded and outlived, so that he or she can progress into the renewal of the future. The attributes of the Fool, joviality and humour, are precious gifts which disperse darkness and falsehood. Use your Cap and Bells to reduce towering demons into the sorry little creatures they truly are! Sachiel, the merry Angel of Jupiter, bears these gifts.

Blessing UNDERWORLD CREATURES *or* SINISTER FIGURES *which haunt* NIGHTMARES

This is simply done, using the thought-form of an undivided, six-pointed star which blazes with a pure white or golden radiance. Hold the dream figure in the heart of this perfect star of divine love, letting it shine in glory from your own heart-centre. Perform this task gently and with humility. It will transform negative situations in both dreaming and waking life.

𝓜AGIC 𝓒ASEMENTS

Appear, appear, what so thy shape or name,
O Mountain Bull, Snake of the Hundred Heads,
Lion of the Burning Flame!
O God, Beast, Mystery, come!

EURIPIDES

𝓣o provide an example of general dream interpretation the most common dream images are listed here with a brief discussion of the symbolism suggested by each. This is not intended to literally 'explain' dreams or to assume a false authority in deciding what any particular dream might 'mean', but is intended as a broad guideline to help dreamers to cast light on to the shadowed symbols of their inner selves, which is what dreams truly are.

○　　○　　○

First of all, it is important to discern the difference between a symbol and an archetype. Jung defined signs in dreams as being less in essence than the concepts with which they deal, whilst symbols are far deeper in dimension, always representing something more than merely an obvious and literal interpretation could yield. An archetype is also a symbol, but one with an objective reality and independent meaning in the worlds within, through which the collective soul of humanity moves as a vast vehicle to which every one of us has unlimited access. If we take the frequently-recurring dream image of Honey and Clustering Bees as an example, we might imagine that honey is a sign that affairs will run well for us; the bee is an archetypal symbol of a sacred force in the universe relating to the mother aspect of the Godhead, a symbol for the Goddess who, through perfect accord, industry and organization, provides an estate for every human soul and for every creature born to the

natural world; and that the fact that the bees are clustering indicates a focus of this Goddess energy, perhaps as a blessing if we take note of the honey as a sign, yet perhaps also sounding a warning that if the energies are misused or misapplied, or allowed to become rampant and an end in themselves, then the bees might swarm aggressively, and give free rein to the poison dispensed by their stings. If the dreamer who experiences the Honey and Clustering Bees image has a business or an artistic project in hand, the dream might inspire them to look at how they are using the archetypal energy symbolized by the Bee, so that a peaceful production of honey might be perpetuated and a negative swarming avoided.

What is there in the dreamer which might tempt him to abuse the energies of the Goddess? The dream might further be interpreted as a teaching on the direction the soul is taking and how it is unfolding its qualities. The archetype and the symbol are the 'magic casements' which will provide these insights, whilst the honey serves as a literal sign that all is well at present, or that the aspiration of the dreamer is sound. Of course, it could also be argued that honey is a symbol for the archetype which is ambrosia, food of the gods! Literalness is never quite a cut and dried business in dreams, because soul wisdom tells us that life is always lived on many levels, that there are many 'mansions' or spheres in creation. There is indeed free scope for sorting dream images into signs, symbols and archetypes. The best way is to rely on your intuition, for dreams are a gift to us, and belong to the dreamer. Which images speak most earnestly and deeply to you, and are a source of revelation? These will be the symbols and the archetypes. Which indicate most literally and seem one-dimensional in their message? These are likely to be the signs. However, keep a look out for the element of surprise even in signs, for it is part of dream-nature to shake us out of conventional thinking!

o   o   o

THE DISTORTED FACE What griefs and fears, anger or frustration are you seeking to deny under a bright façade? Beware of nervous breakdown or nervous collapse by quietly acknowledging your feelings and having faith in yourself to heal them, rather than ruthlessly suppressing or denying them. This dream might warn of false friends, or might be trying to convey that you have received a mistaken impression regarding some person or situation. If the face appears mad or evil, you are confronting some alienated aspect of yourself, which needs to be sympathetically accepted and integrated before it seeks to become a Mr Hyde. The face might simply be fear itself, distorting your outlook on life, or some other goblinesque attribute which is having this effect. Converse with the face and try dream re-entry, carrying back a healing symbol with you. Your dream should then reveal to you how best to deal with the problem.

THE CLINGING ANIMAL This is usually a dream of loneliness. Some part of you feels isolated, under great pressure, and without support, understanding or sympathy. Usually, others in your dream cannot see the Clinging Animal. If it is an ape, the everyday materialist in you is riding your awareness and stifling the freedom of your deeper nature or soul to assert itself and guide you. If it is a snake, the conflict is harming your health. Ask the Clinging Animal to give you a pearl of wisdom in your next dream, and be sure to record all symbols and reported speech when you receive the dream. In waking life, confide in people more, and if they continue to be insensitive to your needs and troubles, take care not to allow their attitude to prevent you from giving yourself proper care and consideration, on all levels.

THE MERMAID Often a strange, beautiful and troubling dream, the Mermaid is usually about your feminine or lunar self, your soul. If she sings, she is warning you to be on your guard against dangerous deceptions in your psychic and spiritual development. If you follow her into the waves, or down to some city beneath the sea, your soul is showing you inscapes of the spirit which you may wish to explore through art and meditation. If the dream becomes sexual, accept her as your lover, because she will bring waters of renewal and deeper life to your sexual self. Ask her for a gift of a song, a poem, a dance, an idea for painting or sculpture, or some inspirational idea for your home, business or project, that you may bring back with you out of your dream and share with others.

THE DWARF The Dwarf is a son of the earth, and may bring you a message from the chambers of the underworld. He may represent some part of yourself you are neglecting, or he may indicate some energy within that you are failing to recognize and so develop. If the dwarf is feminine, it may be your soul, or the goddess powers of rebirth and renewal, that you are denying. More simply, it could be a reflection of yourself, according to your secret perception, and would therefore point towards fostering a kindlier, less judgemental image where you conceive of yourself as having attained full stature, beauty and maturity. Bless the dwarf with a healing symbol, and ask him or her to present you with a gem from the underworld.

THE BLACK DOG The Dog is usually a hound who confronts you. Ask it what it wants. Why are you its quarry? Put on the Star-Drift Robes so that your integrity is maintained, and you cannot be harmed, and instruct the Dog to eat you. If he means you evil, he will not be able to touch you. If he is in himself a healing symbol, he will be able to ingest you into his body, which is your greater self, who has been trying to alert you to claim its heritage by sending the Hound after you in your dreams. If the Dog is negative, reject him as a Dog of Hades, so he will have no power over you, and then transform him with a healing symbol.

THE PURSUER The Pursuer is a similar dream to that of the Black Dog. If the Pursuer wishes to become your lover, firmly refuse rape and take control of the sexual situation. It is healing for the Pursuer to become the Lover. Request a gift from him or her to take back to your daylight self, and if your request is refused, insist.

THE DRAGON The Dragon, always the Great Monster of dreams, deserves the challenge of your greatest adversarial effort and energy, but take care not to begin the fight until you have equipped yourself with a protective symbol, such as the Staff or the Lantern (see pages 40-1). You are fighting for your soul, who is the Chained Maiden. A sense of struggle when wrestling with the Dragon is therapeutic, but if you feel overwhelmed, call upon a knight or another dream-character to come to your aid (see page 73). When the dragon is overcome, you will know that you have transformed the elemental energies of your lower self, and you should ask the Dragon for the Pearl of Wisdom or the Sacred Cup from its hoard of treasure. Bring the image back with you into waking consciousness and see how it translates itself into solar reality.

THE DARK POOL This dream may come to you because you are afraid of being drowned, overcome and lost in the feminine waters of the soul which you feel will engulf your identity. The dream of the Dark Pool could be described as a soul-manifestation of a terrible fear of the Goddess. Alternatively, it could be a threatening but tempting negative mystery which your higher self recognizes it is better not to explore at the present time and under the prevailing circumstances. If you feel this to be the case, summon a star-being and a healing symbol and give yourself up to the waters of the Dark Pool so that you may confront what lurks at the bottom. Bring transformation and healing to this creature, and ask it to reveal to you who it is and what it wants from you. If the Dark Pool is bottomless, then it does indeed represent your soul, or the Mysteries of the Goddess, and you will be transported to other dimensions which will open up vistas unknown to you. Respond happily and with joy to these new worlds, and your fear will be healed.

THE LOVER The most intense and spiritual love can be experienced for dream figures. Be brave and assertive in your sexual union, because this is not faithlessness to your real lover, but an initiation into the sexual mysteries which can then be shared in waking life. The Lover comes to you to awaken the spiritual organs of wonder and reverence in your soul. The Lover bids you seek for beauty, harmony, spiritual meaning and purpose in your outer life, and to cherish the delights of love in all their dimensions. It is always a dream of good omen. Sometimes dreamers experience the devil as a lover; in this case, your higher self might be exhorting you to deal more tenderly and sympathetically with some unharmonized condition or relationship in your life. Love is invariably the solution.

THE ANIMAL ANGEL It has been said of these apparitions that they are a symbol of the 'mystery of being'. If the animal angel is a symbol for the human being, it would be wrong to assume that the animal represents our earthly 'animal' self whilst the angel represents our spiritual and divine counterpart. The mystery is that the angel dwells within the deepest inner sanctum of the animal, whilst the animal resides in its highest harmonized state within the heart of the angel. Without the animal, the angel could not manifest itself. The Animal Angel, then, signifies not conflict, but the greatest possible opportunity for development, progress and transformation. It will appear at a time when we need to be reminded that we truly bear the inspirational powers of the Godhead within us, and can therefore make our lives a marvellous arena of creative possibility. It is a good idea to re-enter the dream and converse with the Animal Angel, asking it why it has appeared to you at this time, and why it has chosen the embodiment of the animal shape it has assumed. The Animal Angel is a dream particularly worth researching both astrologically and mythologically.

THE STAIRWAY With steady, measured pace, the dreamer ascends the Stairway; this is usually a dream of aspiration to do with the material realm of home, business, career and the intellect. Ascent of the Stairway indicates a happy, purposeful state of mind, with an eager curiosity and appetite for what life brings. To run up the Stairway in terror might mean that you strive after advancement in your career, or social position, because you fear that without such a label attesting to personal value, you would be proved inadequate or even worthless. These painful feelings drive you as cattle are driven. If this is your dream, it also involves the Pursuer. Ask the Pursuer who it is, why it pursues you and what would happen if it caught up with you. The Pursuer might be your own self whom you have refused to love and respect. It might warn you of imminent illness, mental or physical, which would strike if the Pursuer did catch up with you (self-destruction). Use a healing symbol and harmonize the negative situation in the dream, and try to carry your new approach through into waking life.

If you are fleeing down the Stairway, you may be giving up earthly advancement in order to seek sanctuary, or running away from the rational level of consciousness because you have not allowed your moonlit self its right to exist and express itself, or because you feel safe if you retreat into the subliminal depths of yourself. You may become lost in a world of your own, unconsciously choosing isolation, or the Pursuer which forces you to retreat might push you into dark, uneasy aspects of yourself. Again, question the Pursuer and seek the wisdom of this dream-figure, invoking a healing symbol in re-entry so that the troubled condition within can be transformed. If you are descending the Stairway, or ascending it, and wake up before you reach your destination, re-enter the dream and continue it, writing down the flow of dream action until your purpose in the dream is resolved and your destination realized.

THE SINGING MOON This is a deeply significant dream of life and death, and of childhood. Listen to the song of the Moon, and it will reveal to you your deepest delights and fears, the whole pageant of your childhood legacy in all its vivid forms and colours. This is precious and secret information indeed, so record every detail faithfully in your

notebook on waking. Remember that the Moon is the gate
of birth, death and rebirth, so these themes bear their own
message for you also.

THE UNSEEN PRESENCE This might emanate threat and be a
source of great fear, or it might be an invisible centre
inspiring feelings of awe and reverence, stirring deep
passions which are indirectly sexual and adoring. If it is
negative, treat as for the Pursuer; if positive, command the
Unseen Presence to become the Lover and enter into the
sexual mysteries to the point of fulfilment, asking the Lover
to bless you and to entrust you with a gift for your waking
life. If the passion the Unseen Presence evinces is not sexual
but rather religious in its fervour, ask it to give you a vision
so that you might understand it better, and learn from it.
To actually converse with the Unseen Presence when it
appears to have mystic qualities can sometimes reduce and
betray the experience – it is better to seek a kind of heart-
to-heart telepathy.

THE UNDERWORLD This sphere is usually recognized by its
atmosphere rather than by means of extravagant imagery
(although this does sometimes occur). If it seems oppressive,
it is important to press on though the Underworld. In
dream re-entry, summon a healing symbol, a protective
one, and don the Star-Drift Robes. Call also upon an
accompanying dream-figure to be your guide, and to help

you to win through. Command that you be ushered into the presence of the King of the Underworld, so that you can converse with him as to the purpose of your journey, the nature of the Underworld, and how you can free yourself from it. If the Underworld seems a place of great beauty and mystery, explore it whilst retaining your sense of wonder. Ask to be taken to the Queen of the Underworld, and request from her its great secret. If she indicates that you are not yet ready to be told, ask her for a promise that you may be allowed to return in the future. At the appropriate time, your dream will recur.

THE STEEP ASCENT This dream, unlike the dream of the Stairway, is about a difficult spiritual struggle. It indicates a personal journey of transformation where birth into the new self is always hard won. Let the dream encourage you, because the constricting outer circumstances it reflects have a beautiful purpose, and cannot ultimately overcome you. If you are visited by this dream, it is particularly helpful to set the symbol of an angel above and below yourself upon the mountain path. In dream re-entry and continuation, see the angel below you as the Angel of Mercy, ready to help you if you stumble. See the angel above you as the Angel of Victory, and allow the dream action to carry you forward into the welcoming arms of this angel, who stands upon the Peak of Attainment and Self-Realization. In this way, you will dream your future waking reality.

The dream of the Steep Ascent is always helped and blessed by the magical presence of Capricorn. Summon the strange Goat-Fish as your help-meet in dream re-entry, because this sidereal god, the spirit of Pan, or the divine in nature, knows with a wisdom as ancient as the stars how best to climb to the mountain-top.

A CABINET OF CURIOSITIES

And he dreamed, and behold a ladder set up on the earth, and the top of it reached to heaven; and behold, the angels of God ascending and descending on it.

GENESIS xxviii, 12

*T*here are a number of herbs which are anciently associated with dream journeys, dream tidings, and lucid dreaming. One teaspoonful of the chopped herb in a cup of hot water (poured over the herb when boiling) taken as a tea on retiring should be effective in each case. The herbs can be mixed, but it is advisable to use in total no more than two teaspoons to one large cup of water, when using a combination of herbs.

o　o　o

HERBS *for* DREAMING

Heather sprigs (flowering), Lavender, Passionflower, Primrose leaves, Peppermint, Mulberry leaves, Cowslip leaves, Sage, Mignonette, Wild Lettuce, Dill, Loosestrife, Dried Hops, Valerian, Mugwort, Corn Poppy (one ground seedhead), Elder, Laurel leaves, Cornbind, Chicory, Lime leaves.

o　o　o

HERBS *to* BANISH NIGHTMARES

Betony, Golden Rod, White Deadnettle, Vervain

In the last instance, take two teaspoons of honey and a few drops of neat cider vinegar in the herbal infusion.

PRECIOUS STONES *which* EVOKE DREAMS

Amethyst, Crystal, Pearl, Olivine, Sapphire, Moonstone, Aquamarine, Diamond, Emerald, Opal, Topaz, Jade, Turquoise

(The jewel must be worn next to the naked skin all night, preferably bound around the head or on a silver chain around the neck.)

PHASES *of the* MOON *for* DREAMING

The time of the new Moon, full Moon, and the dark of the Moon, are said to be beneficial for dreaming. The times when she passes through the signs of Pisces, Cancer, Scorpio, Libra, Gemini and Leo, are also considered to be fruitful moon-seasons for the dreamer (each 'season' lasts about sixty hours, as the Moon completes her passage through the zodiac once every month).

DREAM DAYS *and* HOURS

St Agnes's Day (21 January)
Imbolc (1 February)
Candlemas Day (2 February)
Valentine Eve (13 February)
Lady Day (25 March)
Good Friday (Friday before Easter)
St George's Eve (22 April)
St Mark's Eve (25 April)
Walpurgis Night (May Eve)
May Day (1 May)
Last night in May
Midsummer Eve (23 June)
Lammastide (1 August)
St Faith's Day (6 October)
Hallowe'en (31 October)
Samhain (1 November)
Christmas Eve (24 December)
New Year's Eve (31 December)

○   ○   ○

The best hours for dreaming are 7-8 o'clock in the morning and 11-12 midnight (Merlin's Hours) and 5-6 o'clock in the morning and 9-10 in the evening (Luna's Hours). The hour before dawn and the hour after sunset, at any season, are always good for dreaming. Troubled dreams come during daylight hours, especially after twelve noon. Tibetans call these the 'daylight demons', which hate dreams. An old charm against these attacks runs:

Now do I petition Sophiel
To keep my sleeping soul from hell.

Vervain is placed at the four corners of the bed (a few leaves upon the covers) and a cross within a circle traced in the air before settling to sleep.

SAINTS, GODS *and* MAGICAL BEINGS *which bring* DREAMS *and* VISIONS

St Columba, St Ambrose, St Bridget and St Catherine are said to bring visions. Hypnos, god of sleep, and Morpheus, god of dreams, as well as the Moon Woman, Luna, preside over the night and its visions. The Cockatrice, (the snake-bird), the Griffin, the Unicorn and the Mermaid are totem creatures which dispense dreams. Hathor, goddess of mirrors, is also Mistress of Dreams.

Spell to Evoke the Power in a Dream

Dreams are often imbued with life-enhancing and transformative power. An ancient spell to evoke the power in the dream, to be used before sleeping, is recited to Sesheta, goddess of Inspiration:

Sesheta, Great Goddess! Fill me with your Knowledge,
your Power, your Abundance!
Behold! The Word is born in my heart!
I am filled with Life!
I write Words of Light upon the air!

This supplication to the goddess will help you to bring wisdom back from your dreams, and act out their inspiration in your waking life.

FAIRY FOOD

The ancients believed that fairies could influence human dreams. There are many reported incidents of people lying in a comatose state, sometimes for years, whose souls were often encountered by locals with psychic vision who saw them dancing at a distance on fairy hills in company with the Little People. Occasionally, someone with second sight would stumble into one of the Fairy Halls, and find his or her neighbour imprisoned within (though invariably well looked after) whilst the inert body of the prisoner lay in a charmed sleep at home. Such captives would often exhort the friend who had come across them by chance to beware of 'eating the fairy food' so that they too should not remain ensnared in Elfame or Fairyland. 'Eating the fairy food' seems to be synonymous with taking a drug, either physically, as is more common today, or through the psyche, which consists of entering so deeply into the fairy worlds that the soul isolates itself from the steadying gravity of the earth, and becomes lost in a deep, endless dream.

Many people experience being offered food in dreams. This can sicken, seem real or insubstantial. Whilst no single interpretation can claim a monopoly on the truth, it is interesting to consider dream-food in the light of these folktale experiences (always given as historical incidents, not myths or fancy). If the food offered in a dream seems to sicken and provide a sensation which is the opposite of nourishment, it might be an indication that that which most deeply involves and preoccupies you at the present time has a grasp on your psyche which is harmful and threatens in some way to enslave you. The solution could be to distance yourself from the arena and give yourself a chance to become more poised, dispassionate and in control until a long-term direction suggests itself. If the food seems real and good to eat, this would point to a happy and positive outcome of a current project or involvement. If the food seems insubstantial and unreal, the indication is that what you are pursuing is a phantom, or that you are building a mental or emotional structure upon a baseless assumption, either because someone has seriously deceived you, or because you are deceiving yourself.

DREAM MAGIC

There are several methods to employ in working with dreams, drawn from the culture of the Senoi 'dream people', a series of isolated communities in the central mountain range of the Malay Peninsula, from the Sioux and Iroquois Indians and many other 'primitive' societies. The methods suggest ideas for wielding the magic of the dream so that it can bring harmony, healing, insight and transformation to the dreamer and his or her community.

○   ○   ○

The American Sioux Indians believed that the criminal, the social misfit and the insane were so because they suffered from the attacks of evil spirits which haunted and sickened their dreams. The Bushmen of Southern Africa hold a similar belief and seek to cure victims of social inadequacy, not by isolating or punishing them, but by attempting to drive away the demon of the dream. The entire tribe joins in the effort. This warm and humane method, emphasizing acceptance and integration, is almost invariably successful. It also corresponds with Plato's idea that a 'wild beast' roams about in us whilst we sleep.

The Iroquois Indians believe that dreams reveal their truths
by stating the exact opposite of what is or will be so. To
discover the real truth of his or her dream, the Iroquois
record in detail everything to do with the dream in
question, isolating the incident, attitude or wish being
conveyed, and then acting it out either realistically or
ritually. This is considered a strong spell to bring about a
positive outcome. The images on the totem pole, which
have to do with the special 'story' of the clan, depict
animals and spirits from dreams from which the story is
derived. For the Australian aborigini, an animal appearing in
a dream is the representative of a god, who invests the
dreamer with power through the presence in his soul of the
dream animal, and so it is adopted as a special personal
totem, especially by the healers of the tribe.

The Dyaks of Borneo believe that the magic of the dream is carried over directly into waking life. If the members of the tribe dream that a gift is given to them, they pick up the first natural object with pointedly strange or beautiful characteristics that they see, as a token from the dream-gods. They take it to bed the next night and ask for a dream to advise them in their business, artistic, emotional or health affairs. If the dream comes, the object is treasured as a magical inducer of dreams; if the dream fails to help, the object is discarded and another opportunity is awaited.

○ ○ ○

The American Blackfoot Indians call upon dreams to help them construct their communities. Their holy men have to make dream-contact with the gods before they can be initiated as priests, and their medicine men are instructed through dream-visitations of the witch-doctor ancestors of the tribe. The Sioux Indians would wait entirely alone in a 'vision pit' until their dreams directed their future course in life. The key to dreams seems to be expressed by the biblical quote 'Ask, and ye shall receive'.

○ ○ ○

The Ashanti people of West Africa also believe that a dream reverses reality in order to reveal a truth, but they believe this is done symbolically. If, for instance, a prominent member of the tribe dreamt that a snake swallowed a domestic animal, they would interpret it as meaning that illness threatened their community, or that marauding enemies could be expected to creep up on the village, perhaps at night. The image is signified by the snake's silent slithering belly.

Some of the beliefs of the Senoi dream people, as reported by Kilton Stewart, are deeply fascinating and innovative, and deserve our consideration for practical use as dreamers. They involve the idea that all people can master their own dream-cosmos and call for help and enlightenment from the dream-figures who people it; that unpleasant anxious dreams can be transformed into dream experiences of felicity and spiritual power by wilfully changing fearful responses into attitudes of love, acceptance and self-assertion; that the dreamer should always attack and kill hostile entities in dreams, calling for help from dream-allies when needed, so that alien forces are converted into friends; that sexual dreams should be allowed to progress to orgasm, and a gift requested of the lover in the form of dream wisdom, a story, song, poem, skill or idea so that it may be taken through into waking reality and shared with friends or the community; that a person's adventures and experience in the dreamworld are to be shared within a sympathetic group so that the resultant gifts and problems can be enjoyed or resolved; that negative attitudes and actions expressed in dreams by the dreamer should be reversed in outer life, so that bad or submissive behaviour towards another in dream life can be compensated for by good and assertive actions; and that negative and dangerous waking situations can be healed and transformed in the dream-state, which will then affect outer life so that it becomes a reflection of the choices made in the dream.

I have personally found it helpful not to 'kill' negative dream-figures, but to use the Lance of Consciousness, which is a dream-weapon that pierces through the thick outer hide of the attacking creature so that the healing light of the spirit, or evolved consciousness, can flow into it. This action also calls forth the Knight, a mystical Arthurian figure who appears to protect, guide and redeem the dreamer and the assailant. In whichever direction the Knight rides off, some connecting symbolism occurs so that this wise path can be identified in outer waking reality, and the Knight's guidance can be delineated and subsequently followed.

THE SILVER SEASONS OF THE MOON

In a dark tree there hides
A bough, all golden, leaf and pliant stem,
Sacred to Proserpine. This all the grove
Protects, and shadows cover it with darkness.
Until this bough, this bloom of light, is found,
No-one receives his passport to the darkness
Whose queen requires this tribute. In succession,
After the bough is plucked, another grows,
Gold-green with the same metal. Raise the eyes,
Look up, reach up the hand.

VIRGIL

*T*he Moon, mistress of dreams, rules the tides of earth life and our dreaming selves. As she waxes to full and then wanes to those 'dark nights of the Moon' when for a day or two she becomes invisible in the heavens, she also takes a monthly voyage through each sign of the zodiac so that she completes a 'moon-year' every month. The Sun takes a solar year to move through the twelve signs of the zodiac, with its four seasons - spring equinox, summer solstice, autumn equinox and winter solstice. The Moon acomplishes this in four weeks rather than within four seasons, and her silver seasons are the four moon-tides which mirror perfectly the Sun's equinoxes and solstices; therefore the 'month' or 'moonth' is actually a reflection of the greater year, and might be called a 'Moon-year'.

o   o   o

We too reflect this seasonal round, because each day corresponds to the silver seasons of the Moon. Our morning is the spring, our afternoon the summer, our evening the

autumn and our night, the winter. This subtle
correspondence relates to our lunar, dreaming life, because
as our days move through the Moon Woman's silver
seasons, our dream-sequences are affected. These are often
completed within the space of a month, or dreams of the
same sequence may come at the rate of one each month.
Dreams when the Moon is waxing, tend to demand positive
action and realization in outer life; dreams at the time of
the full Moon are likely to be prophetic in nature, and will
open the doors to psychic sensitivity; dreams whilst the
Moon is waning are often dreams which call for some kind
of banishment of negative conditions within and without the
dreamer; and the dreams in the dark of the Moon can
usually be translated into mystic, secret experiences which
illuminate·the theme of death and rebirth. Whilst this is
only a general guide, it will be found that the more
dreaming is developed as an artistic expression of soul
forces, so this inner pattern can be traced more clearly.

○   ○   ○

Whilst there are twelve divisions of the zodiac in the solar
year, the Moon measures the same time in thirteen divisions
of a little over four weeks in the fifty-two weeks of the
year, so there are always more than twelve, yet never quite
a total of thirteen 'moonths' in each passing year. There is a
magical, hidden zodiacal sign, occuring in May (the month
of the Goddess) between the interlinking tenancies of
Taurus and Gemini, which is described as Arachne, the
thirteenth zodiacal sign of dreams, magic and the inner
mysteries. Arachne sits in the mid-heavens, a spider in her
mystic web, which is the cosmos. Arachne's golden or silver
thread is the sacred cord (symbolized by the revered girdle
of the Druids) which guides and controls the soul-life of
humanity, and is associated with the Celtic Moon goddess
Arianrhad, who holds the silken reins of the subtle inner
worlds in her hands as a symbol of the power the Moon
wields over our lives – a power which, according to the
prophets and seers of our own time, is by no means fully
understood as yet.

CHECK-LIST *for incorporating* ASTROLOGICAL *awareness into* DREAM INTERPRETATION

1. Study the twelve astrological types.

∘ ∘ ∘

2. Make a Zodiac workbook and record all the symbols for each sign (the flowers, herbs, trees, colours, animals and precious stones associated with each constellation).

∘ ∘ ∘

3. Learn the mythology of the planets (i.e., the Sun is the centred spirit, the Moon is the wandering soul, Mercury is the messenger, Venus is the lover, Earth is the Great Mother, Mars is the warrior, Saturn is the marker of time, Jupiter is the dispenser of benevolence, Neptune is the mystic dreamer and rules matters connected with the sea, Uranus is the overthrower, planet of change and energy, and Pluto is the planet of death and rebirth, of buried treasures and secrets in the esoteric sense. The mythopoetic

legends of the planets reveal the inner mysteries of life, and as we acquaint ourselves more closely with these, so their essence will enter and deepen our dreams. For instance, the dove, the sparrow and the swan are birds sacred to the goddess (and planet) Venus. If any of these appear in your dreams, might it be that they are bearing a message from the goddess of love? It may not relate necessarily to sex or romance, but to issues concerned with art and your own creativity, or to an aspect of your life which needs the warmth of love and the grace of acceptance. Other symbols in the dream would need to be meditated upon before a decisive answer could be reached. It is not a case of always attributing the drama and script of the dream to direct experience of the mythic gods, but rather allowing them to speak to you, offering insight, guidance and prophecy, as you tread the magical pathway of the story of your dream.

○   ○   ○

Another example is that of a woman who dreamed of the sea at a time in her life when her spiritual awareness was being directed towards her inner depths, and those of life itself. As well as other images, she saw one dead fish upon the shore, and another far out at sea, a silver dancing form leaping in and out of the waves. She was a Piscean, and it seems that Neptune was speaking to her here, showing her that to concentrate on the earth or the dry land (rational everyday consciousness and material things) would lead to the death of her perception and progress, as symbolized by the dead fish. Her real destiny at this point in her life was to venture far out to sea and explore the waters of the soul, as signified by the silvery, leaping fish which danced amidst the waves. Such dreams illuminate the significance and value of collecting the symbols and story connected with each star sign and planet, so that dream imagery can be interpreted with a new slant and a deeper symbolism.

4. When working on astrologically aware interpretation, consider your own star sign, and the astrological conditions of the moment as your main pointers.

5. Choose an easily locatable star and develop a loving relationship with it. Spend a few silent moments each night in contemplation and communion with your star. If you enter a dreamlike, meditative state, you will find that you can speak with your star and receive a flow of response by writing down the words which come to you. You can speak to flowers, trees, rivers, clouds, stones, birds and animals in this way. Communion with the moon and the stars especially tends to inspire and vivify the dreaming process and its images, lending to them an unfleeting poetry and deeper wisdom. Esoteric lore teaches that the stars initiate their own patterns in each of the kingdoms here on Earth, human, animal, vegetable and mineral. They weave webs of creation out of their own bodies, using the power and life-force which emanate from themselves. All the stars and their planets revolve around a single great light or heart in the universe, which is divine intelligence or God. This holistic view shows us that all life is a magical unity.

The inner mysteries of the stars affect our soul-nature and its development as directly as they initiate the great tide of life which sweeps its majestic way throughout the universe, inspiring the myriad manifestations of creation. In our dreams we are closer, more open to an apperception of these wonders beaming down from the stars, and as we learn from our dreams and bring their wisdom into our daily lives, so our daylight selves will gain a deeper and more beautiful understanding of life in all its starry dimensions!

When you enter the dreaming state with a purposeful bent towards acquiring dream wisdom, invoke the protection of a spirit-guide in the form of a star-animal or a star-figure relating to your own astrological sign. Your ruling planetary angel, who will dispense knowledge to you according to her complete understanding of your need and her wise judgement of what is safe and beneficial, can perhaps be summoned all the better with the help of the magical presence of the star-beings. It is our imagination, inner stillness and receptiveness which together may help to draw us close to the angels.

○   ○   ○

The star-beings to summon (unless you conceive of them differently) are: the Ram with the Golden Fleece for Aries; the Bull of Light for Taurus (Taurus can also be the Celtic Dun Cow, or the Goddess Hathor manifesting as the sacred Cow); the Heavenly Twins for Gemini; or alternatively, two serpents twisting around a white wand: the Celestial Crab, Spider, or the white-winged goddess Isis for Cancer; the Royal Lion Rampant or the Sphinx for Leo; the Maiden for Virgo; the solar deity Ra, or Osiris, god of the setting sun, for Libra; the Dragon for Scorpio; the Unicorn for Sagittarius; the Goat-Fish or the dancing god Pan for Capricorn; the Star-Man for Aquarius; the Two Divine Fishes or the Mermaid or Triton for Pisces. An old spell gives the following directions for summoning a star-being as a guide and protector.

Summoning a Star-Figure Dream Spell

To invoke the presence of one of the magical zodiacal beings so that as night falls and slumber comes the spirit will step into your dreams, you must first ascertain the element of the being you wish to summon. Should that be earth, fetch a stone from the garden. If it is air, the ritual is done by breathing; if of water, a bowl of well or spring water must be collected, and you will need a looking-glass besides. If the element is fire, a candle must be lit. For the spell to be worked, a candle and a looking-glass must both be present, even if your element is earth or air. For fire, perform the working at eight o'clock on the chime; for water, nine o'clock; for earth, seven o'clock; for air, twelve midnight. The angelic hours given are all evening hours.

○   ○   ○

Light your candle upon the hour, and gaze in silence and stillness into the glistening depths of your looking-glass. Call upon the angel of the air, earth, water or fire, and set your radiant candle so that you can see it plainly in the mirror. If you are working with air, breathe in and out three times, slowly, and feel the power which is breath. If your element is fire, pass your hand three times sunwise around the candleflame. If it is water, sprinkle drops from the bowl three times around you in a magic circle. If it is earth, grasp the pebble firmly in your left hand and chafe it three times with your right. Look into the mirror, and let your soul take an abysmal path into the heart of the glass. Form the shape of the star-figure with your imagination, crafting it also with words spoken aloud. For example, you may say 'there stands the Maiden, dressed in white, with a green girdle encircling her waist and a flower in her hair', or 'I see the Star-Man appear, clad in robes of blue and gold, bearing his Cup aloft. His mantle of eagle feathers is thrown back over his shoulders and he rejoices all the eyes of heaven with his sapphire-eyed beauty.') Then you may say:

> *Maiden who is Virgo, heed my prayer;*
> *By gods of water, earth, fire and air,*
> *By Rulers of the Elements, Angels Four,*
> *Who Gabriel, Michael, Raphael, Uriel are;*
> *By spirits of the elements, the named Four*
> *Who Tharsis, Kerun, Seraph and Ariel are;*
> *I bid thou, star-being, appear in my dream!*
> *Summoned art thou for this night's theme.*

Call the figure you have created in your imagination into your future dream three times. Then snuff out the candle and make sure you are abed within the hour.

Arachne, the magical Spider, or the Spinning Goddess, is a wonderful meditation-symbol for dreaming. Try creating your own artwork of her and contemplating it quietly. You will be surprised at the vivid impressions you are likely to receive from your subliminal mind. As queen of dreams and the inner mysteries, Arachne can be called upon as a healing and transfigurative force in dream re-entry, or even, as our dream-power grows, in the midst of the dream itself.

Similarly, the Moon herself is a beautiful meditation-symbol
for the gift of dreams and the magical granting of insights
into them. Without constriction, try to abide by the silver
seasons of the Moon and their dream influences when asking
for a particular dream (visionary, waxing; prophetic, full;
healing, waning; mystic and transformational, dark of the
Moon). Of course, all four types of dreams can occur at
different seasons, according to their nature and purpose.

○   ○   ○

Seek out the Moon, or Arachne the Spider, when you are
alone in your room, or, even better, if the night is fine,
take a walk to some lonely place where you can view her
clearly, and make your request. Luna's silver visions of the
night can be transmuted into the alchemical gold of day-to-
day living, so that Yeats's paradise can be realized, where,
'till time and times are done', we pluck the 'silver apples of
the Moon, the golden apples of the Sun.'

$\mathcal{I}$NDEX

List of Spells